# Poems in Our Absence

## by Claes Andersson

### Translated by
### Lennart & Sonja Bruce

With an Introduction
by
Bror Rönholm

Bonne Chance Press

FIRST ENGLISH EDITION

Publishers Cataloging in Publication
*(Prepared by Quality Books Inc.)*

Andersson, Claes, 1937-
  [Poems. English]
  Poems in our absence / Claes Andersson ; translated from Finnish
by Lennart & Sonja Bruce.
    p. cm.
    ISBN #0-9638398-5-3


  1. Andersson, Claes, 1937- --Translations into English.  2.
Finnish poetry--20th century.  I. Bruce, Lennart.  II. Bruce,
Sonja, 1919-  III. Title.

PT9876.1.N35P64 1994          894.51'13
                              QBI94-1387


1 2 3 4 5 6 7 8 9 0

# Introduction

Claes Andersson is a man of many roles: author, psychiatrist, jazz pianist, member of Parliament, leader of an opposition Party, candidate for President of Finland; Finnish-Swedish, middle-aged, a lover, and father.

All these are relevant to his poetry. Andersson believes that human beings are whole and indivisible. He is a socially conscious poet, who emphasizes that what we are, we become together, shaped by common internal and external factors. "What is important," he writes, "is not what separates us, but what unites us."

Andersson's 1965 attack on the aestheticism, preoccupation with nature, and introversion of the modernist tradition in his journal *FBT* was also an attack on a narrow and antisocial view of humanity, and on the self-pitying feelings of isolation and powerlessness of a minority literature. His own writing—urbane, "dirty," straightforward and clear—strove to expand radically the range of poetic motifs and language, to expose the ideologies that control us and the ways language conceals these instruments of power. His social criticism went hand in hand with his criticism of language.

Andersson's poetry is founded on oppositions and dialectical affects—beautiful love poems juxtaposed against the poverty of a homeless person or a mental patient, objectivity leavened with irony, black humor, and verbal playfulness.

In the seventies, Andersson started to allow the musicality of language into his poems. Earlier, he had shied away from the excessively beautiful and "poetic" as almost dangerous; now, he began to open his work more systematically to dreams and intuition, attempting to incorporate and develop the poetry of metaphor he had favored in his youth. From this point on, one can distinguish two general strains in Andersson's poetry.

The first uses private life as the foundation for an investigation of all that shapes our identity and determines our existence as individuals and social beings. This aspect, which feeds on Andersson's experiences as a psychiatrist, draws a sympathetic if melancholy portrait of human beings as vulnerable and entangled in a sticky web of dependency and unyielding structures.

This may account for the undertone of joyful surprise when Anderson celebrates the unexpected spontaneity and freedom in the harmony of Nature, the uninhibited freshness of children, poetry, music, the golden moments of closeness between people, and, of course, love—impossible and life-giving.

The other strain is a continuous poetic and critical commentary on our times and society in which the poet reacts with seismographic sensitivity to shifts in the cultural climate. The two strains are intertwined: there is no boundary between the public and the private.

These days, to be whole and indivisible is a central project of Andersson's poetry. Increasingly, Andersson as poet and musician succeeds in including Andersson as psychiatrist, politician, and fellow human being in a free, relaxed human existence; the different voices meeting in a dialogue that allows a variety of languages to enrich and unmask each other, often resulting in images that are both contradictory and suggestive of multiple meanings. He puts it this way in his 1985 "Thesis." "Poetry creates a new reality. It is not merely imitative... Literature changes reality by changing our view of it."

**Bror Rönholm**
*Nordic Poetry Festival Anthology*, 1993

# Poems in Our Absence

## by Claes Andersson

What became word in me
were traces of something forgotten
that I had seen your lips mumble
in the half-light of the adjacent room

It starts with our meeting
Meeting is essential — not the two people
                                    who meet
Your hands are open
I open my hands to you


        "Society's smallest unit is made up of two people"


Inside our cells
there's a strange half-light
That's where the poem is born
I call what happens there  o s m o s


            It happens in every direction and at the same time


When the wall is ruptured light rushes in
Life rushes out
We're born, and simultaneously in every direction


                We have a date tonight
                We shall meet tonight  wall against wall
                I listen to your whisper:
                without walls I'm lost
                without walls we're lost
                without walls you're lost too


"The migration of substances through semi-permeable
                                    membranes"


                We press against each other
                hard, harder
                my wall tight against yours
                tight, your wall against my wall

When our walls break light rushes in
Life rushes out
It happens to us
It happens to us in every direction
simultaneously

Do you remember how our worlds while mumbling
    slowly slid into each other, occupied each other's space and
      became one world.
Do you remember the living dream that woke us
    in the sleeping world, and all that came
      because it had to come.
The flowering of your skin, your inverted face in me.
A crow perched on the tin roof that saw everything.
I should have gone home but was home already, I
    remember that's just how I remember it.
Through spine's marrow and the ribs, happy and blind.
I saw all.
We tumbled as though unattached, with
    arms around our arms
      like flower baskets.

Already as a child I loved someone like you.
Sleeplessness then made me sleep away
my best days.  Nights I spent regretting having lost
forgetfulness.  When dawn approached it came
in the guise of a woman.  She kissed me with her tongue
of light.  She kissed sand under my eyelids and
I stayed awake my eyes smarting until the night
returned with its clear anxiety underneath my skin.

Butterflies worry me, they're pretty, fleeting, they
are like Eve. I cannot fall asleep with them. I
treat them badly, chase them away. I become
violent in their company. When you've driven them away
you see them everywhere. One of them is in the floral print
that covers the garden seat.
One flutters over the kitchen stairs. One
disappeared into the mouth of the sleeping child. One
sits calmly on the lover's bottom during coitus,
grooming its wings. One guides the lost one
to a new wild strawberry patch. One has its belly full
of them. And one catches the eye of everybody
while the wedding goes on out on the landing, in the storm.
Nobody sees anything else when the priest shouts
"will you take," inaudibly. Nobody sees
anything else when the storm blows the bride away
across the ocean of sin and she floats suspended
like a cirrus cloud through the wedding rings of the rainbow.

We caught a glimpse of so little of all
that was given to us
So little we managed to keep of all
that was taken from us
Where did joy go — she who generally came
uninvited, followed by her sister Anguish
in her skirt of bandage gauze?
Who butchered the sexual urge? Entombed
in a wrinkle?
And yet! Those rare moments
of presence! The tropical birds! Kingfishers!
Golden Orioles! Bee-eaters! Fleetingly beautiful creatures
barely touching our skin, they barely got a taste of
our blood before they were gone again
plunged into the same depth from which
they had been thrown

## A dream

I cast my new lure, the crocodile one
I got a strike almost at once, something big
I pulled at the reel, and my knuckles whitened
Then at the end of the line:
something limp and heavy
I pulled in the catch and saw
it was my own dead body as a child
My hair was white, with bangs
Eyes blue and wide
I cut open the belly  It smelled good
from cinnamon-baked apples and new-baked bread

Grandmother had climbed up on the spleen,
sat there knitting
I said hello to her, crawled into her lap
She read me "The Pearl of Truth" by Z. Topelius
Then she sewed up the ventral skin
Together we jumped back into the sea
I felt happy as never before,
a sense of security

Despair is far too big a
word, but I don't know... Because sorrow is
incurable, it never heals
Thus its strength, its fruitfulness for whatever
hasn't been destroyed within you as yet

Whoever hasn't got sorrow has nothing
Whoever hasn't got sorrow might do
anything!  To anybody!

Whoever hasn't got sorrow has never lost
anything, never had anything
The hurt and the appeasement doesn't exist for

the one who never had sorrow.  And the poem
grows only out of sorrow, the sorrow
that has been given refuge in the hub of joy's wheel
and there been purified to become vision and forgiveness

(to Mother)


Did we know each other?
Was it you who gave me food and held me in your arms
    when I was little?
Were you the one who made the fires and kept the
    beasts away?
Unnamed, you named me,
    your namesake.
You shaped me with your lips, your kisses
    gave me birth.
Your glance became my telescope, I learned
    the universe of the face, and of the stars.
Your hands carried me.  You bore the burden.  I was
    your uplifted one.
When much later I became someone to myself
    you were inside me.
When I saw myself I was unaware that it
    was you I saw.
We were part of each other, everything your image.

(to Father)


You're bleeding inside, your strength is running low,
    your anxiety, your care, your love.
You were no good at handling feelings, they were too strong.
Is your car OK, you asked when we met.
Then I knew it was about love, collisions, dents,
    the countryside rushing by,
      driving under the influence, speeding,
        war and fuzzy images of childhood.
Now that you've grown smaller I understand
    that enormity of yours
      which once scared me shitless.
You smoked like a tugboat, healthy as a horse
    the shovel of your hand. Your heart of steel-plated gold.
I, once your son, have become your father.
Stop bleeding, let go of your wound.

I write to you
to get a glimpse of the little
boy who never cried although
he was as full of weeping as a
bucket of frozen water.  After
winter comes winter and no
warmth is expected.  I'm freezing, I'm
frozen, but if I
thaw I'm pulled into the earth.

This is one of those times.  Something
ends, irrevocably
Something else begins
unavoidably, impassable?
It's time for a good-bye
and for all good-byes

It's time for breaking up
and to stay.  It's a time for
new visions, a new giddiness
It's the time to miss and to give up
all that one has missed, the joy and
the lack of it, a time to give them both up
There's time to touch once more
those one loved, the living and those living in memory
It's the time to give them up and to
give up one's relinquishing
It's a time to cool and to be set on fire
into a blaze a thousandfold greater
This is one of those times

## A little boy

A little boy's father stands in the garden outside his house
sawing firewood.  It's the beginning of June and the sun feels
warm already.
While sawing he thinks of a little boy's mother, right now
on a trip to Italy.  He's also thinking
of a little boy who left a little while ago on his bike
for the gas station close by.
A little boy's father is sawing and still has no premonition
of anything.
Then suddenly, a cloud covers the sun and a cold gust of wind
from the north with its chill hits a little boy's father from
behind and he stops sawing.
He puts away the saw and sees somebody on a bike
coming at him at great speed down the hill.  And that
somebody yells at the top of his lungs.  A little boy's playmate
yells from afar: he was hit by a car.  A little boy
is under a car.
A little boy's father at first feels unreal and cold,
as if thrown into an ice-cold well.  For a few seconds
reality is totally unreal.  A little boy's companion stands
screaming tears running down his cheeks and
down onto the ground covered by sawdust.  "The ambulance
came and took him!  There was blood everywhere!"  A little
boy's playmate stands screaming.
A little boy's father jumps into his car and drives, wheels
screeching to the hospital two miles away.
He rushes into the emergency clinic.  An ambulance with its
rear open stands swiveling its blue light.  A little boy's father
rushes up to the emergency window screaming, my boy!
Where is my boy!  And he runs through a long corridor and
kicks open a white door with the sign Surgery.

A little boy lies on his back on the examination table. His head
is bleeding. His eyes are wide open and he is
somewhere far away. A little boy's father leans over
him and calls him, but a little boy sees nothing
and hears nothing, while blood slowly trickles from his ear
and mouth. A doctor in a white smock is busy sucking up
the blood coming out of the little boy's nose, ears and
mouth.

A little boy's father drops to the floor, and is spared
the sight for a while.
When a little boy's father wakes up he sees a white ceiling.
He rises and asks for his little boy, but little boy
isn't there anymore, a little boy has been transferred
to the neurosurgical clinic in the city. A little boy's father
jumps into his car. As in a dream he drives to the city and the
hospital where a little boy has been taken.
A little boy lies motionless on a table. There is
almost no blood
and a little boy appears immersed in a deep sleep.
A little boy is fast asleep and a little boy's father
watches by his bed.
A little boy's mother is in Italy and still knows
nothing about what happened to little boy.
For two days and nights a little boy's father watches
by little boy's side, who just sleeps and hears nothing
sees nothing.
After two days and nights, long as a lifetime, a little boy
opens his eyes and sees and a little boy's mouth mumbles
the little word: dad!
And a little boy's father sees a little boy's eyes and hears
the word and then at that moment he knows
that the summer outside

will go on, that the grass will go on growing
and that the bird-song
will go on and that the wind will blow through the fields and
travel the crowns of the trees also this summer.
A little boy has returned after a long journey and
from that moment on a little boy's father knows that there is
such a thing as grace and that there's nothing to fear
any more, not in this life nor in any other life.
And six weeks later a little boy's father carries a little boy
in his arms and puts him in the back seat of his car. And a
little boy's voice says: "Dad, drive to the store. I want an
ice cream."
A little boy's father comes home to his house. The saw lies
there just as he left it. And he goes on sawing
where he had stopped.

Man loses his light in his shadow,
is carried away, wakes to the smell of coffee, black-
bird song, woodpecker's hammer, green leaves
shining  brightly between the bars.

The sky becomes water's image,
the water sky's image,
bird becomes fish's image,
love light's image,
dream hope's image,
death death's image.

In our love hope is reborn that we
may not be forsaken, rehearsal is
in progress, we learn nothing in life.

Sometimes I might be struck by a sudden certainty
that this very instant harbors some significance,
way beyond all other instants, yes that this
instant within it contains all other instants.
This feeling rarely lasts for long, perhaps a second.

Nothing can deprive us of our memories.
Except habit.
Except the unwillingness to drag along miscellany.
Except the sleep and the calcifying.
Except faithlessness.  When Sisyphus goes on strike
the rocks start rolling.

You could have spared me
the humiliation there is in having
too little of everything. You seem
to lack all respect for what is nothing.

We see each other only
through the cracks in
our faces
Summer is the season of death
There's so much life then
Death is oblivion
suddenly called to mind

Come let's climb the birch tree together
high up to the top, making it sway
under our weight, and we're flung
two dandelion seeds under one parachute
plunged into the lake's shuddering mirror
We float together without
a stitch on our feelings
We let ourselves sink to the bottom and make it
our home, for a while
Among wizards artists and alcoholics
we hear sirens play the violin, out of tune
like a drowned Gypsy string band

Rock on my waters.
Drown in my waters.
Let sleep take you on my waters.
Weep in my waters.
Come to me in my waters.
Dissolve in my waters.
Loosen your hair in my waters.
Become you in my waters.
Become no one in my waters.
Become someone in my waters.
Become my waters.

## Etude for summer wind

She walks with the wind in her hair
I love the way she walks
I love the way she walks
with the wind in her hair
I love the way
the wind moves through her hair
and the wind's way
of moving through her hair
I love when she walks
I love the way she walks with the wind in her hair
I love the wind's way with her hair
I love the way the wind moves through her hair
I love her
when she walks with the wind's way of moving her hair
I love her and I love the wind
when she walks with the wind in her hair
and the way the wind loves her hair
I love her when she walks with the wind in her hair

## Villa Biaudet

The house had a red-brown, ancient color.
It was imbedded in greenery, almost hidden
behind apple trees, birches and a huge elm.
Vines climbed up the walls of the house.
Inside the rooms there was a greenish light
when the rays of the sun filtered through the foliage.
There was a  nice smell of books and clean dust.
The owners had just left the house
for a long journey.
It was like being handed a gift from times past,
to hold on to it for a while and link it
to our own time, our own lives.
There was a feeling of joy starting to work with the words,
remember and shape the future
out of the past's weave of the now.

## State of things

Your face is so alive when you laugh.
your soul is so beautiful when you speak.
Your love is so timid when you make love.

You sleep, tired from the day's work.
Exhaustion and the news keep me awake,
Our child laughs in his sleep after the day's play.

You say something is ruined between people.
You say that the groundwater has been poisoned.
You say there should be something other than
                              the fear and the hate.
Other than the fear and the hate.

They haven't crushed us.
You are not alone.
Where there are two of us alone
there's no longer one alone.

What are you saying:
that hate without a direction is despair,
that sorrow with no object is emptiness,
that love without a tomorrow is desperation?

Behind our words exist realities like morgues.
What's unalterable can hardly be formulated.
What happens without words we shall reinstate
in the language.
The poem is a redeemer.

Nearness is invisible.
What you have behind your eyes
you'll never see.

When you speak it's like warmth.
I hear the separate words.
I listen to the warmth that ties them together.

To drive a person insane is easy.
Deprive him of everything.
See how strangely he acts.

He seemed to act strange
with a wry and somehow awkward grin
submissive and servile
During the coffee break at work
he was silent most of the time,
acted strange
He could just as well get fired!
Joining the unemployed
or lazy as they say
They started to call him bum, s.o.b.
Then he began to act even more strange
eyes shifting and squinting
movements jerky
Somebody had seen him alone in the woods
just sitting on a rock staring
Then he even walked with a stoop
a little lopsided like some animal in hiding
Not quite right in his head for sure
They put him in an asylum to be on the safe side
He got lots of pills
Now he is really sick they said
Reality became covered by a sticky film
He started to behave even stranger
just lay on his bed stiff as a stick
chain-smoking
He got more pills
Reality got stuck altogether
He was transferred to the ward for chronics
Well, what did we say, we said

Whatever happens to be suffused with light
becomes visible
To write poetry is to change the light
so that also the shadows become distinct
so that also the trees' subterranean crowns...
Unlived words obscure
The ones lived carry vision
Someone walks with a lamp through the dark
There in the dark are all the other ones
who now begin to see, yet are invisible
The hidden ones
I want to write for them

I slowly lift the lid of my box within boxes
They are all there
the women the kids and the summers
the scents of resin hay and manure
the memory of a wind with gentle fingertips
An unnoticeable movement through it all
as the big truck passes the oak in the courtyard
in the middle of summer and the leaves
shiver all at the same time without falling
Kids play in the grass
their mouths open and close
and a summer hymn heads for the open waters
in an open boat with all sails set
The water is clearer, more transparent
than the sky above
It opens downward inward, like memory
Here was a ground
where the perch stood still as sticks
I've been here before
The fish tank is full of dead fish
mossy from age as Brahms
I turn my eyes inward and search
Pulse beats, rhythmic contractions
waves that come and go as at childbirth
ejaculations, orgasms
From straight ahead the eel is hard to tell from a mouse
Sure we long for the past
but which way is back
when the directions lie scattered in the grass
like wild strawberries
Last summer the clouds lay low
I groped for them as if for udders

Mother's face was obscured by the clouds
The sun blew forth and colored they bay green
after a quarrel
A war broke out in the portable radio
rattled through dad's face
He fell silent and in a couple of days he left
Nobody dared ask him when he would come back
But the mushrooms remained shining
in my glade
the ants chattered as usual
the butterflies were muted by their own beauty
Everything was unchanging changes

(to Tadeusc Rózewicz)

Among the felled trees of the forest
he looks for a place where
the birds may perch

Among the flowers in the clearing
he looks for a long time before he eventually
finds the features of those gassed to death

The cat that rubs against his leg
does so merely because it happens
to be somewhat smaller than he

During his long wanderings
he met many people except
the dead who were everywhere:
she who had forgotten everything
she who never could forget anything
those who always spoke of something else
Those who said nothing, said nothing

A fully dressed man, umbrella over his head,
walks into the sea until also the umbrella disappears

He takes out the picture of the gray mud-field under a gray sky
A horse lies dead, hitched to his plow
Few remember that picture any more

He practices death
learns the features on the inside of his face
He slashes his nape, from the front backwards

A stench of urine and beer when he cuts open
the belly of the whorehouse and the dead walk
in and out through open doors

Breathe breathe life!
Blow through my numbed faces
through my shriveled love
through my torn feelings
Blow through the rooms where I sit withered
jammed into a book
There's nothing as degrading as the word unlived
life's disgrace and the hand
without an aim for its movement becomes a talon
dragging across dead things, the unkissed
mouth becomes an acid hole
for the intake of sustenance and for slander, so breathe
breathe life!  Through my longing until it becomes spirit
and flesh, through my bitterness
until it becomes regret and appeasement, blow hard
into the stillness in the eye of the storm
Blow through the old woman's quiet dignity through the scenes
that turned yellow and faded on  her journey, through
the shift worker's sleeping hands, stirring holding his tools
also in his sleep, breathe through the bureaucrat's house
of dandruff and papers, through the evacuated face
and evicted stare of the homeless

Blow through the high-rise's swaying nooks where
the many thumb their little pill-boxes of forgetfulness, blow
through our cages that we drag along filled
                                with guilt
through the lysol-stinking holes of neglect in the asylums for
the insane, blow through the young girl's
supple heart when it's been forsaken, through
the child's clenched fists that never learned
another way to long for love, blow

through the sealed lips of those fallen mute
so that the language again is transformed into weapon and
solace and open hands to hold on to, breathe breathe life!
through the deserted shack where the field mice run
through the nettles, through the vanished paths
where curious children once ran barefoot toward
the beach, blow through the big city's tightly buttoned
anonymous overcoats, through the prisoners
                                    and their
imprisoned keepers' sadomasochistic clinch, blow
through our walls and frontiers, our night-
                                    mares and
restrictions, prohibitions and amputations, blow
through all that inhibits and obscures
ourselves and all others equally obscured, equally
full of possibilities to be freed
in spite of all!

(suburbia)


Deep inside the concrete wall
a little girl's laughter flares up
without any warning!
The concrete starts cracking
The apartment building sways
My idea of a high-rise tumbles
and unexpectedly unveils
its living garden
in bright oil-colors
they veer about on their small bikes
You can barely count them all
It's spring although it's the season of fall
          and the heart is as brittle as concrete

We only have this miserable life
so filled with joy and pain
and ice-cold nights
So full of farewells
So filled with work
and ice-cold nights
with somebody breathing
close by our shell-like ear
There exists a trust indivisible

The stone in the bird
falls wingless  We
fall through each other
through our hidden
eyes  Stillness is seed
spilled in the hands of dawn
To whom do we belong?
Birds of leaves  Birds
of stillness  Birds of
loneliness and possibilities

(Chopin, a dream, 1966)


Please be seated here by the grand piano, play dear Frederic
— it was my wife's voice!
The A flat major Polonaise was flung in cascades
                              against the walls of the heart
You play gorgeously, not like a human
                              almost!
— my wife's voice again!
He asked me to take out the stethoscope
                              was it consumption?!
I asked him to play softer while I listened
The examination showed no sign
                              of illness
Would you like some coffee and cake?
— my wife's voice for the third time!
We felt like real people in Frederic's company,
                              so natural,
so relaxed, how true he seemed
You should have heard him play!
He played like no one before!
Glittering waves at play on the shore of the heart!
Cascades of light and agility, reflections from the light
of his genius, and something else, beneath the surface,
                              something tremendous, magnetic,
deadly, relentless, barely discernible, passionate,
                              emphatic,
blood-black, sacred solemnity!

Jazz makes me wild, my clock stops.
At a concert I fell off the stool
   in my piano solo of Wild Man Blues.
Malicious tongues wagged about aquavit. Bach!
It was the jazz, the slave's revolt.
I can sit all night talking to Thelonius
   Monk, his madness is tritonic.
My wife thinks jazz is too American, our president
   prefers Finnish tango.
The secret of jazz is that you never know what happens
   next, just like in football.
Lovemaking is often dull, introduction, main topic, epilogue.
Jazz is never dull.
Musicians are a special breed, first you think they're
   dazed, eyes glazed over, getting drunk.
When they stomp off the Milestones one grasps the profane
   width of the word holy.
Some never learn to play.
They pretend, drive huge cars and tuck the dough in their
pockets.
Jazz becomes a dependence, like morphine, politics or
   the stock exchange.
Once hooked, you're stuck, ruined, happy,
   crucified.
The ingenious jazz musician dies young.
If he survives the car crashes he goes insane, takes overdoses,
   or jumps off the balcony,  These Foolish Things!

Do become more of a seed more mirage
Become flow of force flow of love
Blow hard through the room like brass music
Vanish as dandelion fluff in the horse's mouth

In Helsinki buildings aren't very attractive
The parks not very green
The air not more polluted than in other big cities
People not happier than elsewhere
Helsinki is a city without a face, with
a faceless smile toward the sea
The whole city is mostly nape, back
Sometimes one imagines a smile
from the back of the head, laughing with its posterior
Then one tries desperately to run around to the
other side to catch a glimpse of the eyes, the mouth
The city stoops low then, sweeping the fog
tighter around its shoulders
One may love Helsinki for its
plainness, for the lack of features on its face
its indifference to those
who drop to the pavement of the streets
and remain lying there

## Short break in life

How was it?  How have you been?

Unstable.  Black-edged clouds.
Gilt-edged caskets.
Many or few people at the funerals.
Turbulences with epicenters of love.

On these latitudes the day comes fast
    and unhesitatingly as the woman I love.
And I'm totally confined.
The hibiscus is on fire, high heels flee across the market place.

Quiet.  The hot stones in my mouth must be allowed to cool.

A platoon of Spanish-speaking sea gulls are lined up for
    orders on the playa,  they intend to attack the silvery
    fishes pulled in with the nets.
I might be one of them, winged, with scales.


The earth rolls away underneath me as I run, coupled
    to the Huge Wind Machine.
A baby blimp from some child's domain floats in
    from the sea, lands softly among the dunes.
Bird craniums, quills, jaw bones, chunks of cork.
And they're gone, the dunes wander on.

I'm staying temporarily on a fifth floor balcony.
Every day same time the cleaning woman enters the room
    and sweeps away my memories.

The table is empty for a few moments. That's all the gravitation
a human can take.

I take a break

I step aside and watch us flow by, the children
   aging as they walk about, someone comes to a halt
   and falls while newborns appear and are taken in
   accepted by the others.
For a second I stand watching myself as I walk
   with all the others.
Wolves.
Faces, elbows, lips bitten into, excrements, residues
   of wings.

Everybody knows that each one knows that we're on our way
   toward some kind of ocean and before that ocean
   there's some precipice.
The ocean's water touches bottom in our water.
We feel it touching bottom inside us, rising, sinking...
High tide, low tide... low, high.

I lean over the balcony railing, almost plunging
   crushed against the pavement, break my neck, see my
   face pressed into my nape.
Black cats frolic mating in the grass, hard
   to count, four or seven.
Tiresome: to write away the words that are obstructing
movement.

Short break in life.

Down there, the youth in rags, malnourished, infectious, dirty,
  with the silver-gleaming stereo underneath his arm!
To fly out, pulled out over the waters,
  catch a glimpse of the playground of the blimps, be inside
  the wind machine, high on breathing, light, dry like
  the jaw bone in the sand.

In huge stray pale flocks people
find their way here to vacation-land
The longing for warmth and closeness brought us here
but it's rarely up to expectations
Everything has such a funny taste
People here don't understand our language
Somebody ordered meatballs but got squid on his plate
At first he thought it was a joke
Then he understood they looked upon him as some idiot
Surely the waiter hadn't even been in the Winter War
So the squid was thrown in that grinning face
Hell, it wasn't he who should pay
Tried to hit one of the cops, spent 24 hours in jail
Came to the hotel pale and harrowed, sat down
and wrote the postcard home:
Everything just fine. Food great. Bought an umbrella.
The weather varied. Trying to really relax. Don't forget
to phone the plumber. Hug and kiss. Dad.
We walk along a windswept shore,
condoms floating in the water
One recognizes the palms but not the other trees
There are supposed to be sharks here too
and thugs who slit your throat in the alleys
When the plane touches down on the runway back home
we applaud
as if we had seen a smash hit movie.

(Sjundeå, July 1978)

These bright trees, these
bright words across the spread on the table
under the aspens, those bright
words protecting the distance from one
to the other so that the real becomes
plain beyond our images of longing
that we carry with us down to the well
of sleep where we accept our natal
predestination without fear, and
right now the horses stand in the clearing
completely still, I view them
through the web of arteries in my hand, they
don't move, a sudden heavy steaming downpour
stops and the rainbow appears
We stroll underneath the trees and clouds Today
we walk under the cloud-trees and speak slowly
inward to ourselves about the simple things
to touch

And all the time
death proceeds with trivia's
entropic inevitability, sperm
penetrates the membranes
of the seething armored vehicle, the dead
soldiers are fertilized
The egg cell in the bomb-sight is attacked
by atomic warheads, it dies and
starts to multiply with insanity's
speed, the sea
strikes into the uterus, fuses with
the water of the amnion and the unborn fetus
is pushed through the hot vagina, the child
wakens on the steaming shore where traces
of humans are still
clearly visible.

A free man also has the freedom
   to limit his freedom.
Love is freedom limited.
A precipice, the freedom to step over its edge.
You're my precipice.
No one knows how steep it is, I'm falling.
It's like ascending.
Heavenly meadows pass with their flowers.
I touch your blossoming body.
I'm free inside your body.
Nobody knows how deep you are in your body.
We're falling, ascending, blindfolded free.
We fall into and away from each other, feather in stone.
Stone-heavy feather, stone-heavy stone, we lose ourselves.
Whatever ends goes on in the blossoming, in
   its precipice, ultimately.

With your dark side
you push me away from you
With your bright side
you pull me close to you
You lock me out
You captivate me
I'm torn in two halves, the One
wants to be inside you, the Other
wants away from you
The wound bleeds in two directions
When the closeness becomes too poignant
it suffocates me
When the distance becomes too great
it suffocates me
I am the wisp of hay between the two stubborn
mules Hate and Love, one a cursed
copy of the other, the damned likeness
of calf and heifer

I hide deep inside
my sorrow, my love sleeps heavily
after betrayal's epileptic assault
The doldrums' sounding-lead pulls me toward the earth
and something in me wants to get away, be
grass and trees with wind and light
in their crowns, become light and swiftly
passing birds, away from my being
that sits here clawing the page, to
the undemanding world of sand, the undemanding world
of light that no one sees and knows and asks

We know so little about birds
because they always flee from us
You hardly dare hold a dead bird
in your cupped hand before
throwing it into a close-by ditch
Everywhere everywhere one imagines then
that one recognizes the dead bird, among
one's friends, among one's
friends among the clouds, among the clouds
it seems one recognizes
the dead bird held
in the cupped hand same as
a tiny living young bird

## Guilt

Blood gives off a scream and someone falls.
The victim barely gets time to feel the taste of blood.
But already before the dandelion in the cemetery
has flung its first parachute
the murderer also loosens his grip.
Together they sink toward the earth.
The grass starts to breathe again.

There's no peace in life.  Scent of stone, it weighs
and carries.  There's a rising rain inside me and I
would flee but am myself every possible location.  Call it
God or Pepsi, whatever there's missing, but don't mislead me.
Don't speak of what's not there, and if it ever was, has
ceased to be called by that name.  One evening when nothing
is missing I notice that the ongoing party doesn't
concern me.  I take my name and enter the night.
Soon the music will cease, soon the laughter
won't be heard and
the streetlights will fade like flares in fog.  I don't
remember those I forgot, the party goes on but I'm
not there and nowhere else.

Loneliness is a pyramid, human stacked
upon human, a barracks crowded
with sleepless monologues
The shadows get longer toward evening, people
squint at their old age, an eclipse
behind tinted glass
They're blinded one last time, fall upward
toward the sun before they freeze, snowed in
through the heavy door of the hospital
The diagnoses are scratched into their skin
Everything melts, left are only their smiles
that quietly tell us
about the solitary flower of death

In memory of an air crash

In the plane that caught fire they dreamed so heavily
that their dream didn't change
although the wings fell silent and burned.

Snow is falling on the site.  So gently
that not even one snow flake lands there, with its chill.
It is dangerous to wake up now.

The fuselage is gone and so are the wings
they used as they approached and dared the world.

Who ventures to tell them what happened
while they were asleep.  What happened?

They gather in surging flocks before bidding farewell
and head across the boundaries.

Across your oceans with waves like wrinkles
Across your shores with grains of sand like pores
Across your waters with lakes like eyes
I leave you in the morning
and arrive toward evening
The places I leave and the places
where I arrive fill me with the joy
and the anguish of rediscovery
My journey in you is complex
takes place simultaneously in opposite directions
Before I fall asleep I recall you
with all the habitats of my skin
Even the parting is a reunion
The distance brings your closeness with it

To love is to respect
the independence of the one loved
That's how I see love
Where the hell is she

(last poem)


Come let's hug, the wind is terrible.
Mourn me when I die, don't remarry ever.
At least not with Kurt or with Burt.
Don't wear the miniskirt to my funeral.
If there's to be music it should be Tannhäuser
with Pavarotti and Birgit Nilsson live.
I leave all the parking fines for you, my scourge, to inherit.
Hope we won't meet there.

Close by and everywhere
the questions appear
like heavy snowfall in adverse light
Violent like a hailstorm
the answers strike
I try to think of all
now living people
simultaneously
Then your face appears
you, who isn't closer to me
than I can bear

There's a loneliness that rarely leaves me
Nights become drizzle and little children breathing close by
In a way we get younger as we age
and learn the alphabet of the face anew
learn to read the wrinkles around the mouth
spell the furrows of the brow
What we keep quiet about is whatever can't endure
the butcher knives of the words
Both of us know that we know where we've put them aside
Loneliness and silence are twins: not identical
but symbiotic like moon and sun
To be born is to be cast out
We haven't accepted it altogether
That's why we can go on

Each surface has an inside
as feeling is the inside of language
and oblivion the one of memory
and the one of oblivion death

The words like the elements possess hidden valences.
As when the word Natrium jumps into the word Water
to cool off, without suspecting the result of its leap.
Thus the hidden tensions may be revealed.

At the indescribable moments when the struggle is still on
a strong light develops.  The words can be read.
That may happen even to two ordinary people.
The poem is a meeting-place for such encounters.

Don't overrate the keeping silent
Speech is a treasure
Rats and pestilence grow inside the silence
Look at the tumor, how it silently eats you
It has no use for a dialogue
Don't believe for a moment that the executioner
    enters into argument with his victim
Do you believe that the malignant growth yells Good Morning
Do you believe that the lack of love confides in you
    disclosing its shortcomings
Do you believe that the bullets quarrel
Do you believe the rope weeps?
Do you believe the sleeping pills sigh?
Don't believe that people write resolutions
    when rats have gnawed the tongue out of their mouths
Do you believe that barbed wire will do for gramophone
    needles?
Don't ever believe that something grows within silence
    except the silence of silences.

Leaves in my eyes, earth
in my mouth, I love the trees my cousins
with rain in their hair, the screened
green light in the aspen cathedral
sways me like a polyphonic fugue by
Bach, the trees have no age, they have
visible and invisible personas, their
subterranean hands work in the dark
fields where the dead rest after
life, the photosynthesis proceeds polyphonically while
we bring in the harvest among honeybee scooters
and bumblebee copters, with the useful
tools in our hands

(Philemon and Baukis)


If you become a fir
I'll be a birch
Thus you protect and warm me
through the cold seasons
In return I'll dance for you
in the summer nights so that you get the strength
to bear the melancholy of your roots in the frozen soil
Then both together we become more
than each one of us, a mutual
concern and a joy shared
so that we get the strength to continue our work, the growing
here among all that abandons and threatens
when the birds have left us on a charter
in lighthearted flocks away to the southern bird-centers

We set traps for the animals, we caught the birds
   in huge nets.
We were the chosen, chosen by us.
We lay waste the forests, burned the vegetation.
We turned on ourselves, tore the heart out of our
   bodies, clawed and tore at intestines and genitals.
Dug out our eyes, gnawed at our bones.
Our hunger grew as we ate.
What kind of chronic disease is this, what kind of hunger
   is eating us while we eat ourselves.

I want to hide unconditionally in your
timidity and invoke the light
like someone born blind, and you:
a torchlight in the subterranean passageways!
When we now meet underneath the
gorgeous light below the tall
trees' autumnal calm
I want to hide one and all
in your timidity

The sorrow smoulders in your eyes
slowly night falls in our embrace
as if we were the two last animals
In the night of fall we sense the scent
of our common sorrow in our breath
Life is heavy breathing, as if somebody
dragged his childhood up to the attic, yes,
as though somebody tried to hide his childhood
away from time and sorrow, from the wind
that chases away the smoke from the huge extinction-
                                       furnaces

## Friendship

1.
I don't know why I like you so much
Maybe because you're without a skin, your
lack of cunning?
I want to change my ways toward you, through you
But what if my shell breaks, what'll I do with all its pieces?
Two people stripped of their skin, will they come too close?

2.
I remember an autumn when everything had almost died
You seemed as happy
As one feels when something has finally come to an end

3.
Sometimes you giggle and it sounds like crying

4.
It was very cold at the bus stop
You wore something ridiculously furry
The bus came and we hugged, I felt
the heat burning inside you
You left and stored your warmth in me over the winter.

5.
Andersson is out of his mind, you said cheerfully
when I considered taking my life

6.
Often you were scared
I saw it in your eyes that lost their foothold

and plummeted from tall bridges
Sometimes I managed to catch you in midair
All went back to normal, the caring
back to normal

7.

We both suspected reality couldn't be relied upon
That gave us a funny feeling of trust I believe
we rarely abused
But it put us at rest, the bird we had in common

8.

We often talked about children, of their ability
to remain in the present, all the time.
When sometimes they fell ill, they became like us, as if
they were not quite where they should have been

9.

When we were separated, traveling
we never sent postcards
Nothing had to be confirmed between us

10.

It was generally enough if one of us read a book

11.

It happened that we both got an impulse
and phoned each other at the same time
Then the line was occupied
Weeks could pass and there was no need to try again

12.
We both loved the summer, we never saw
each other then
We were both out of our minds

13.
You gave me huge radiant chunks
of my reality

14.
We never said we loved each other, we knew
all too well where the ropes and gags were kept
It was our kind of defense

15.
We did some things together
we never finished
That way they never ended

16.
Now I've gone crazy, you said over the phone
I didn't want to interfere
I knew you were deep into something
The plug was pulled

17.
Sometimes we got staggering drunk,
A mutual confidence
We quarreled as if our lives were at stake!

18.
I remember the feeling of loss
when I first met you

of all the years you had been absent in me
You didn't want to be chosen, yet
you chose me
It's a desolate road, but with people lining it
What are we waiting for, was all you said

19.
Without you the poem would be somewhat more unreal

20.
Without you life would be somewhat more unreal

21.
Without you the unreal would be somewhat more real

It was the summers we remembered, always the summers
We got lost in them, they became a kind of fixation
Autumn evenings we leafed through all the photo albums
where the kids grew taller from year to year, like sunflowers
to eventually blossom out of our pictures
The voices of our summers, our summer voices turning green
through the long summer days, the meals outdoors in the
garden, remember?
                              Yes, yes!
On the veranda we planned the coming summers, all the
changes we would make
                              and how we would paint...
Summer kept us alive all through fall, winter and spring
As we waded through mud and slush it kept us alive
When we went to work pitch-dark mornings, when we
returned home
                              in the dark
the summer shone like a lamp inside our bag
It was summer when we met and fell in love, summer
when we made love in the grass, sure it was summer!
Our children were conceived in the warm summer nights,
all our pale
                              March children
If something went wrong, something went awry we consoled
each other with the summer that soon would come
Some summers it was rainy and cold
Then we sat in our summer house kitchen freezing, read books
                              and drank tea
In an exceptionally rainy summer, we just said
The summer has such a power
It is a miracle
If we were religiously inclined we would have no other gods

## Poems in our absence

Your absence attracts me
I shudder at the thought I might discover
a streak of submission in your eyes
I constantly leave you, so
you'll let me stay.  This far on my way I know
that every attempt at escape is nothing but
a change of prison, an instant spell of dizziness
as we plunge between the tension of bars, our longing
We're being pursued every moment, overtaken
and then abandoned, the war of containment goes on
ceaselessly in the trenches of our skin, in every pore
of the concrete wasteland we inhabit, as an inebriation,
the rapid flare of a dream was the moment we lived,
in the 'status nascendi' of disintegration and delivery when we
were abandoned and gave ourselves away for another, unknown

The long periods of absence.  Where was I
during the daily roll calls?
Absent.  Away.  And your absent body
like a shadow on the wallpaper of the hotel room
Was I inside you then?  Did we meet?
No.  I was absent:  hardly noticed
the children climbing in and out of my lap
like up and down an old oak standing mute, withered, a
ghost in the woods, paralyzed in the sad
mumbling between roots and crown
Not even inebriation brought me closer to myself, not even
the dream made me become more visible
My journey was too much of an escape.  But our shadows
coincided and imprisoned us, a shadow
of something past which came painfully close

One day the older children stood like giant sunflowers
looking down at me
Wake up Dad, please!  We need you!  Who?  Who
is needed?  For what?
And in the most natural way, the child who once
was the youngest, the most loved one, threw his arms
around me and I became a child again, became present
in his closeness

It happens that fatally wounded we get caught
like hooks inside each other, the more we struggle
to get free the deeper our injuries
We grow old, elbows hooked arm-in-arm
like a folk dance couple on a still photo
from days gone by

Like watching a movie
when the film suddenly breaks
and neither stamping the floor nor whistling will work
because somehow you're paralyzed
and because you don't know whether it's you or
the picture that has become invisible, that's
how I felt when you left me for somebody else
Then, when you came back I felt nothing at first
and after that, an all-consuming joy,
all-encompassing hatred
Meantime somebody had swapped movies
Now they were showing a cruel and technologically
advanced war between small children, who all had
somehow grown together
I tried to tear loose my hand but found
it was your hand, and that the one sitting
next to me wasn't you but I

(the falling in love)

We crashed into each other, fell through bedsheets of
light which rendered us invisible to each other, we
were flung out from the ashes into the fire. Everything
that might have become reality in that border zone where
growth and withering clung to each other, all tied
us together and made us beside ourselves
We knew it
We didn't know it
As always the truth was revealed to us in the dream:
Our hands fumbled through slivers of glass, the
chainsaws of our caressing hands, the bubbling gas chambers
of our capillaries, blood gathering, engorged exaltations
To talk about it feels threatening, but under the heaviest rock
there was an inverted tenderness
We were in a car without a driver, seat belts fastened
traveling at high speed
There was a roadblock, we never saw it
Something struck the windshield and our faces
were smashed in a flash
The road was closed, impassable
A life scenario in progress with headlights put out

I caught a glimpse of you where the Nose Pucker Trail
crosses Mouth Corner Alley
It happened some time during the day
I got caught in the little crease that appeared
just there when you smiled
An empty bed came rolling down the slope
It was just jump in and let go
In many ways it became a simple journey
We reached the sea at sunrise
Seagulls were hung out to dry against the azure-blue sky
There was the house we'd dreamed of
You were more eager than ever
Small children appeared in the corners, with milk teeth
and wailing sounds
I had never lived in a birdhouse before
It was a cramped existence
When winter arrived we chopped up the bed for firewood
Perhaps that was shortsighted
We had to sleep standing up
At the family therapist you didn't agree with me
Just like morels and the sand
You can never get completely rid of it
Its crunching between your teeth drove me crazy

At first you promised nothing
Then you kept the promise you didn't make
Then you promised never more to deceive me
Then you betrayed me (you had promised nothing)
I swore to be faithful from the beginning
I betrayed you
It had never begun
You got raving mad
You changed your mind about it all, promised anything
I've betrayed you, I said honestly (to kill you)
You went back on everything
You deceived me, definitely
I got furious, tried to kill myself
I tried to betray you
It wasn't possible any more
I wasn't I any more
I had become you
I couldn't betray myself, in you
We lost all that we'd never cared about having
Thus we had lost everything

I lay awake beside you and
was happy in the dark
You were asleep   The dove
slept with its head under the wing
I didn't dream of a waterfall
inside the mountain
I dreamt that I was a tree that
was axed from behind
I fell with my face against the mountain
The mountain was smashed   Underneath was
another mountain   It didn't shatter

You laugh through me
while I fall
Through your laughing face I see
your weeping face
Just underneath it, a face distorted
by fury
Behind them the remnants of a smile
And underneath them all, the semblance of a little
child's astonished face
Through them all a death mask stares
It stares through me out of your
deformed partly dissolved faces

Nowadays I don't trust you any more
than I always trusted myself
As soon as I turn my back you deceive me
And right you are
I would do the same if I were I
Someways I'm not me anymore
I get extended bouts of faithfulness and caring
It's some kind of revenge
Now when there's nothing more to massacre
we could have it fairly good together, you and I
But you!  You don't mean a word of what I say!
Go to hell but come back

We lie naked together on our backs
We've just made love
Saturday morning   The window moves slightly
in the May wind
The birch trees glow faintly
Two programs can be heard overlapping on the old
portable radio, Ravel's string quartet in F-major, and as
if from the far side of a wide field a
lecture on crop rotations
We lie silent listening, your left hand
on my shoulder, my hand cupped
around your breast
You feel cool, unperturbed
Soon the kids will be here, before they disappear

As far as you are concerned all I did lacked intention
There's no such thing as an intentional feeling of loss
nor intentional sorrow
There's no intentional hatred
But year after year my searching for
your face filled my being
It was never revealed to me.  It wasn't there
It took all my time
But meantime; how many ignored glances
rejected smiles!
You tired of my meandering
You left me for somebody else
I was forced to grow  Nowadays I live alone with you
It hurts, otherwise everything is much better
There is no intentional hatred
You don't have to worry about it

I write out of my obscure part
I write the inside of my skin into blood, I write
my face that's taped onto me, the cathedrals
in my fingertips.  And somebody
not visible walks through me, in and out
through the dark archways where the scent of childhood
remains hanging in the silver cobwebs where the spiders live,
the shy baby spiders that love me, that
love my licorice colored blood and
my childhood sweetness that they eat
They run a school
They write me   They write my inner skin
They fill it with spider signs, with letters
and crosses, with words and bites and with holes
through which whoever so desires may view
my childhood lapses that are taped onto it
through the perforated sky

I wanted to write a poem about my mother's
face as I saw it for the first
time forty-six years ago
It won't work
I get no distance from it
I cannot envision it
It has moved itself inside my face

When I was born Helsinki was a medium sized
city with cobblestone streets
A couple of years later the war broke out
I had just learned to keep my mouth shut
Old ladies lay strewn about in the streets
after the bombings.  They tried to kill us all
There was total disorder
One of those frenzied nights when everything went black
mother carried me down to the basement
Then she disappeared, she had no eyes
It went cold and wet and dark
I felt it in my lungs
There was an iron door that was not to be opened
When I squinted the building turned into
a seesaw of cob where all the dead
were hung from long ropes in the basement passage
Right when a bomb hit really close mother
and father hugged for the last time
like in an R-rated movie
Sirens went mad, they entered
my ears through the ear flaps
Dad was gone all the time
although I didn't think much about it
I carried my white cat down into the basement  We sat there
for so long it got blind and ran away
Somebody found it with its head blown off
in a box marked Newsprint
I sure recognized it, I understood
that no one was to be trusted
I didn't cry, was all dry
I kind of elevated from myself
and saw me left lying without a head

I held my breath until my cat was whole again
It never worked
My lungs were useless, I was about to die
We lived in the water under the ice crust
I was a quiet child, I blew the heads
off the rats with my BB gun
It became too difficult to breathe
Something swung back and forth like a pendulum
on the bottom underneath the water
It called to mind what was left of a little boy
in knickers frozen solid underneath the ice

(underworldly, otherworldly)

Starting point. Now. Nature is sparse
in Helsinki, leaves
fall from the chestnut trees
Dogs sniff, the fog
has returned from the sea
Orange-colored men drill their way
into the roots of the city, uncover
tunnels, halls, waiting rooms, bomb shelters, niches
The city is afloat, this is
old marsh land, Ogle
A young man with a white cane
crosses the park, stops in  front of Johannes
church and raises his head, stands thus
for a while.  We listen to the drills
sounding underground before he
goes on, groping his way with the cane
Above his head pigeons ascend and descend
Perhaps he is a holy man, he
may have wandered here through centuries, from
Assisi, perhaps Theiresias is his brother, they
are drilling ever deeper
the city is mellowed by the darkness, slaughters
proceed globally, it's incomprehensible, meaningless, as when
the watch in the tower is without vision:
tracer lights through the dark
and no one sees, no one catches up with them
I pull the blind, put on lamps, lock
myself in with my fear while I work inside
my cone of light, perhaps
he is a holy man?
Dark shadows, as if cast by ascending and descending

pigeons traverse the paper as I slowly fill it
with signs and music: a fugue
of autumn and slaughter across the world
Whose were we? Somebody who remembers? Who remembers
the madness and the slowly emerging
questions? Somebody who reached the sorrow?
what was there? Somebody who reached the end of weeping?
Through the darkness I imagine what I remember:
clear air and the park's flocks of pigeons, the
rare friendship, the incidental
love, the candid children, the leaves' light bodies
over the cloud-reflecting puddles in the park

To be deserted is at least something!
You who were never abandoned, what feeling of loss
do you live from, which want carries you,
what emptiness dreams you!

And all you who were outside
me, who forced yourselves into me, all you
sorted out from my memories!  I
beseech you: Resurge!  Without delay!

Resurge radiant face of Mother, the
one smoothed by tears that remained in me.  Rise again
her distant face, her
warding off that stayed with me.  Resurge
her hands picking birds in me

Rise again the feeling of loss of father's hands there
in the bunker at the Isthmus that remained in me

Resurge strangled great crested grebe caught on
the scissor hook of my trap inside me.
Be resurrected the glazed eyes, the drooping wing,
the lice, the beauty
the terror that stayed in me

Resurge the voice of my aunt thin as silk,
silk being torn, her eyes swollen with weeping in me

Rise again my white blind cat with your head
blown away in me.  Come back the war on the
veranda when nobody was allowed to speak!

Resurge soft rains that remained in me, the
white fanny of the girl astride the canoe, the
light-red slit in me

Come back you huge horses in the pasture
that stayed in me.  The steaming
udders in the barn, the calf's tongue of sand in me

Rise again you German soldier who drifted
and beached by our landing, who
remained in me, his face eaten away in me

Rise again you deformed rats, the intestines
under the heel of the peasant's boot, the white eyes
of the rats looking at me that
remained in me.  Be resurrected the smacking
sound and the blood rinsed away
in the drain that remained in me.  Be resurrected!

I mistrust the invisible
I mistrust the atoms jumping in the air
I mistrust the radiant neutrons, the whole
particle rubbish
Spirits and demons are humbug
But see what you see!
See the bread crumbs that the sparrows and
the chaffinch dance around by the bird feeder!
Real is also the tongue making its orbit
around the sun of my palate
and your hand that quivers like a
sparrow when you sit astride me
I love you as deep as I reach
with every fiber of my fathom line

Steal from us and call it economics.
Make us homeless and call it city planning.
Humiliate us and call it welfare.
Drive us insane and call it mental health.
Poison us and call it environment protection.
Anesthetize us and call it consumer philosophy.
Make us unemployed and call it rationalization.
Mislead us and all it advertising.
Sell our bodies and call it sexual freedom.
Deceive us and call it profit incentive.
Make us materialists and call it standard of living.
Mock our work and call it early retirement.
Lie to us and call it freedom of speech.
Oppress us and call it democracy.

They stop at nothing

Watch out for him who says he speaks
for many.
Perhaps he does.

Watch out for him who says he speaks
only for himself.
Perhaps he does.

Watch out for him who always nods
in approval.
Tomorrow the nod might apply to you.

Watch out for those who only want
to live peacefully.
They stop at nothing.

If someone opposes you kill him.
If someone looks offensive kill him.
If someone stutters or limps kill him.
If someone avoids your eyes kill him.
If someone pushes you on the street.
If someone passes you on the freeway.
If someone is ahead of you in the market checkout line.
If somebody grins at you kill him.
Or at least give him a hard kick
  in the face.

Some people smile all the time, they have a
broken zipper in their mouths
They smile when they talk, they smile when they're not talking
They're one big smile, smiling with the back of the head
They smile their way through dinners and meetings,
they smile in bed
They smile on the john, in the army, at the bottom of the ocean,
                              their wounds smile
Their smile makes people love them, adore them
They smile when they tear off wings from little creatures
They smile at wars, at hunger, straight into the mass graves
They smile at somebody lying in the street
Smiling they talk about future disasters, exterminations
They smile their way across borders, Customs, past doormen,
                              while making love
They smile at each others' smiles
Smiling they accept orders for bigger ovens, better
                              chemicals
Smiling they delete our names from various lists
They're practically incapable of anything else, but they know
                              how to smile
When they leave the room their smile remains
Nothing works, not even airing or spraying
Cutting their smile only makes it broader
It's like an invisible Buddha, nonexistent and yet it's there
Assail them and the reply is a lethal smile
The movie *Jaws* broke all the box office records

Never thaw somebody deep-frozen
  too fast.
Cells would overflow, walls burst,
  the heart would stop.
Never place someone deep-frozen
  in a micro oven.
Put him or her on a hard bed in a room
  facing north, open all windows.
No blankets nor pads, hardness
  is essential.
When calling for water,
  ice cubes will do.
When hungry, offer stale bread.
Never stay in the room long enough
  for the person to get attached to you.
Loneliness, seclusion is required.
Offer a scrap of coarse cloth for cover.
When he or she eventually has regained some body heat
  you'll be told about views of
    rare beauty and barrenness.
Every polar explorer, mountaineer, outdoor enthusiast
  and physician within intensive care is aware of this.

You'll get the wool in the bargain if you take care
of the sheep
You'll have to endure the scream cutting up
the pork chop
You'll have to accept being an outcast if you want a glimpse of
the insight
You'll have to endure the vertigo getting high on
the view
You'll have to take the consequences if you are set on
your intention
If you long for the plunge you'll have to take
the impact too
You'll have to accept the full repertoire if you want
the love
You'll have to accept the bars if you're turned on by
the chasm beyond
You'll have to take the damned equality if you insist on
human rights
You'll have to take the bureaucratic swamp if you choose
the center
You'll have to take down the robbers too if you want to get
Jesus off the cross
You'll have to endure the grief if you wish to behold
the poem
You'll have to get off at the last station although
you only wanted
the journey

Nowadays there's much talk about identity
As always one keeps busy with the nonexistent
We confuse scarcity and longing
One can swallow sharp objects (some do)
like pieces of glass, nails, filings, needles
thus changing one's identity somewhat
One crucifies oneself believing
that way to gain some more presence
There are other methods: charter travel, unconsciousness and
getting stoned, workomania, religion as a
cross in the paunch
Maybe we want to believe, but see no reconciliation
We put our stakes on an afterlife, see before us
souls, souls wandering, soul upon
soul, yes whole migrations of souls. We'll be disappointed
We'll have to settle for simpler forms of life:
some molecules in a blade of grass at the cemetery
a barely noticeable smell from the crematory smokestack
a few crystals in the cold eye of the urn

About my afterlife as a lawn
l can tell the following:
I feel my stubble bristle!
Finally I have a crew cut (she always wanted that)
I love the rains, just like before
No need even to give up soccer
The kids' naked feet tickle my nape joyously
I sleep a lot (my watch was left behind there)
The neighbors are called Bush, Pine and Elder
Long sighing straws run through me
In summer young warm women come and lie down
    on top of me
Anxiety can be felt as a mole loose in my innards
The sun rises out of the Eastern ditch, sets in the Western one
I sleep under the open sky
The stars tick on my bedside table
All talk about grassroots I find laughable, as when
Some city planner was here and measured me
That hurt
Some days it feels as if people peed on me
Earlier I never noticed the wonderful palms of my hands
When the cat eats me I know rain is on its way

(the new theology)

Disease is the conscience of the body
What would we be without our ailments
Many marry them to be
on the safe side
Some advertise: seek relationship
with discrete, well-balanced diabetes
or:
insatiable, well-to-do growth seeks soft bosom
Reply to Yours for ever
Paul Tillich tried to undo symbiosis with group sex
Then death came and took him away, but those were
interesting times, writes his 83 year old widow
The reading of one's blood pressure is also a kind of caress
Some people love when somebody listens to their heart
(the stethoscope leaves the mark of a wedding ring
on the chest)
Elderly men prefer prostate massage
Some teenagers cut their skin with razor blades, the wounds
cry out for love
Our diseases protect us from feeling lonely
We can rely upon them as upon friends loyal for life
You can talk to your illness
You can go on vacation together, to health spas,
convalescent homes
It is like a  p o s s e s s i o n, always with you
Neighbors don't start talking behind your back either
You can love your sickness with at least half your heart

It sounds like snow when we want to scream, it
sounds like snow when we want to weep in the roar of silence,
with our mouths frozen solid underneath the snowdrifts
made up of faces inside the roaring silence
The black rowanberries coagulate on the snow's
eyeballs in the roar of the silence, the needle points
of the white eyes
coagulate in the roar of the silence, the snow
burns us to bones in the roar of the silence

Credo


Despair.
Shared by many
turns into
confidence.

If everybody cries, who'll
then notice the weeping?
If everybody complains, who
will then change the conditions?

The conditions of many
become the knowledge of many.
Knowledge becomes insight, insight
action.

Change is no longer a possibility.
It becomes a necessity.

And whatever became your life
was only partly lived, not lived
to a great extent
Something prevented you
and held rule over you, like Lenin
over the tomorrow masses
Live while you live
Then die

Whatever there was to complain of
  I complained of.


The black glue in my songs
  was called lament.


But inside the black, straws of light!

Weep for the dead who lost this light.
Weep for those who strayed in their darkness.
Weep for us who strayed in our darkness.
Let the rains pour on the dead who lost
    this light.
Let the rains pour on all who were shut out
    from the childish desire to love.
Let the rains pour on those who lost this
    childish desire.
Weep for all who lost this childish desire.
Let the rains pour on all who are shut out
    from the childlike desire of love.
Weep for all who lost this light.

Have you seen a human illuminated from within
As when a lamp unexpectedly is lit in a
darkness in a neighborhood nobody has seen before
It's as if we woke up simultaneously
from a dream we hadn't known
that also everybody else had dreamt

and still when the light has gone out and the face
has sunk in among the shadows it lingers
in us, bears new dreams, more fervent than ever

(friendship, dialogue)


It is from my own experience
I'm able to recognize you in me
I scan you
First for spots superficialities surfaces crusts...
Then layer upon layer
level after level
until directions are no more
You reason inside me
You echo within me
Your voice becomes many voices
Your voice becomes a chorus of many voices
your pain reflects the wounds of many
You become essential
Your life implies the life of many
The deep dialogue transforms and changes us
becomes as many voices as the wind, illuminates
becomes insight
a light refracted
through the unleashed dreams of generations
Our task is to make them come true

## Pathetic prayer

The seed has an inborn power, growth, blossoming
It's harder to blossom in the language
To write a line that's aromatic and shines
is something to dream about
while awake, while waiting and working

Merely to fertilize your own garden patch and wait for miracles
is a means of contemplation for monks and self-centered poets
I join in the seed's prayer: let life
rain on me, let me drift from land to land
on reality's winds, don't let me take root
until I've brought with me a part of the world

A flower so beautiful
that it's out of this world
is only beautiful
and not for this world

Therefore save the flowers for wreaths
Let me drift from land to land
Let reality rain on me
Help me not to take root.

(in memoriam)

She was aflame.  She burned there naked underneath
her burning clothes, without shame, without
despair, without hope, she burned!  She burned
without a word, she burned like an unheard prayer
She burned where the smoke of her eyes rose out of
the graves, she burned in defense.  Her wounds
burned, she burned like a piece of neglect, her
enigma burned, and all her secrets
She burned like the birds' shadows in her hair, she
burned blurred like an ancient parchment on God
She burned on the open sea, beyond all
breakwaters, she was a water-blaze that fire
extinguished, she burned for remembrance and penance
She burned to quiescence in the cheek of the bed sheet,
she burned to the weeping, the consolation, the resurrection
She burned for  the wonder, she burned for mother and
for father, she burned to asbestos
She burned for the inadequacy of our flame

The moment the words are electrified means
everything  And nothing  The roof lifts  Flies
away  It means nothing   Your frontal bone is broken
loose  Flies away  The nose comes loose.  The kneecaps
The brain jelly  The paper lanterns of the eyes
Everything flies away  It means nothing  You are
in the center of it  You're nowhere  You have broken
loose  Flown away  You're holy electricity
Satan's grace  It doesn't mean anything  Your soul
has left you  You don't possess it anymore  The house where
you lived tumbles   You're the roof that lifts   The walls that
tumble  You live nowhere  You're obsessed  You
tumble  It means nothing

(For Joyce Carol Oates)

Nothing exists  One has to
   imagine everything!  Even
this summer, muggy
   as a wake   Also the congregation of
wasps that crucified its gray
   church in the fork of the back room  And all that is
assiduous  Our diligent friendship  Our
   diligent hatred.  Our crucifixion to one another
We must imagine our
   imagining, the distracted contractions
of our sleek muscles during
   the orgasm and the  black grass snake
slithering across the path to the sauna
   like a foreboding this morning  One has to imagine
the resurrection!  One has to imagine
   the rocks that crushed the snake's head and
the ants, their attack, how they ate themselves
   into the eyes and stomach of the snake, death in the snake's
heart, the sluggish contractions that eventually
   ceased  Our faces are assaulted by
the wasps, the children cry, we spray the wasps
   with poisons that kill them  We must imagine
how the poison acts, how it slowly
   penetrates and blocks the nerves'
synapses, we must imagine the paralysis, the
   tiny animals' abstracted contractions before
they're slowed down to finally cease
   We have to imagine the entropy, how
everything successively falls silent, we
   must imagine the life that distractedly
stiffens and leaves us remaining

on a floor somewhere, like
the rag dolls in the playhouse, where we no
  longer can enter, we must
imagine everything!

My dreams have metastasized
My dreams lie dying
The vultures over the Round Tower in Bombay
circle over my dreams
My dreams have been felled and paved over
My dreams are contaminated by truth
My nursery is filled with dead dreams
My boy puts his arm around my dead dreams
My dreams dissolve when he touches them
There's a roaring silence in my dream world
My dreams fall like sprayed butterflies
They fall like leaves in the infant's autumn, millions, gorgeous
My dreams have forgotten the sea that gave them birth
My dreams have forgotten that they had love

Dusk walks through our house, the enigmatic
animals stride out of their hiding,
                              our inner persona
is dreamily outlined and deepens into visibility: yes,
living is still possible as it was possible
before we tamed the words that later became our
tyrants and forbid our sights
We re-conquer ourselves once more, for the last time,
                              while
life abates in us and we pass it on
to the children in the neglected garden

While you try to remake the world
the world remakes you
You've forgotten your dream
This is the tragedy of evolutions
and revolutions
Don't flee from them, then
you become an easy prey
of both
(you'll be anyhow but in another way)

Something dries up withers shrivels
loses its leaves and eyes and fingers
But the root swims about underneath the earth
with its blind happy eyes